CHARTER
AIRLINES

CHARTER AIRLINES

Their aircraft and colours

JOHN K. MORTON

Airlife
England

Acknowledgments

A proportion of the pictures reproduced in the following pages could not have been obtained had it not been for the help given to me by the many friends I have been fortunate to make at various airports around the world. To all these people at Palma, Rhodes, Manchester and Miami along with the United Kingdom-based airline executives who have 'fixed' things for me, and any other person who has assisted me, I thank them and acknowledge their patience and help.

I am also grateful to two United Kingdom airlines for supplying latest information to accompany my own text – thank you Air 2000 and European Aviation, and to the publishers of *Airways* and *ACAR* for information used.

My thanks must also go to my publisher, Airlife, for their assistance in the preparation of this title and for their continued interest in my work.

Copyright © 2000 John K. Morton

First published in the UK in 2000 by Airlife Publishing Ltd

British Library Cataloguing-in-Publication Data
A catalogue record for this book is available from the British Library

ISBN 1 84037 098 X

The information in this book is true and complete to the best of our knowledge. All recommendations are made without any guarantee on the part of the Publisher, who also disclaims any liability incurred in connection with the use of this data or specific details.

Typeset by Rowland Phototypesetting Ltd, Bury St Edmunds, Suffolk.
Printed in Hong Kong.

Airlife Publishing Ltd
101 Longden Road, Shrewsbury, SY3 9EB, England
E-mail: airlife@airlifebooks.com
Website: www.airlifebooks.com

Contents

Introduction

The aircraft enthusiast will already be aware of the differences between a scheduled and charter airline and will immediately recognise one carrier from the other. Although this volume has been produced with them in mind, I am also considering the many travellers who may only fly once or twice a year when taking their holiday. It is to the latter that I provide the following information.

Do you always know which airline or which type of aircraft will take you to your chosen destination? Maybe not. The trip will have been booked far in advance and as long as the airline gets you to your destination and back again you are doubtless quite happy. The majority of tour companies rely on a number of charter airlines to transport their clients to resorts around the world, and the aircraft involved will be specially chartered and configured to carry the maximum number of passengers. This volume illustrates and describes some of those airlines and, hopefully, will put the nervous and timid passenger's mind at rest when he or she walks along the jetway to join his or her never before heard of airline.

During the northern hemisphere's summer months, a large proportion of aircraft are in service for up to eighteen hours a day and the flight you board will not necessarily be the only one it will perform that day. However, a regular programme of servicing and maintenance is performed to ensure a troublefree flight.

During the winter months your aircraft will probably not operate similar services to those performed in summer, and to achieve maximum utilization of what is an extremely expensive machine to operate, the airline may lease its aircraft to other companies around the world for alternative use. There are instances within these pages where aircraft in the ownership of one airline are providing flights for another country's airline during the United Kingdom's quieter periods.

I hope this volume will provide the information you have not previously had the opportunity to find, and throw a new and different light onto your future inclusive tour travel plans.

The all-inclusive tour business and airline charter companies are constantly changing, with smaller organisations being taken over to be merged into their larger counterparts. It is therefore possible that when this volume is published some of the airlines included may no longer be operational.

JOHN K MORTON

Airbus Industrie A310 C-GCIT was the second airliner with which Air Club entered the charter market. The twin-engined A310s operated the carrier's shorter flights within Canada and the US, one American destination being Fort Lauderdale, where the French built airliner was photographed about to land in December 1995.

Air Club

Air Club International, a Montreal-based international charter airline, commenced operations in June 1994 with an Airbus Industrie A310 and a Boeing 747. The carrier's first routes were to the United Kingdom, shortly followed by flights to the Hawaiian Islands from points on the west coast of Canada. The airline has currently suspended operations but intends to re-start in the future.

Boeing 747 C-GCIH, one of the first aircraft to enter the Air Club fleet was photographed about to depart Frankfurt/Main in August 1995. This airliner made several flights 'over the pond' during the mid 90s, and was also a regular visitor to London Gatwick and Manchester.

Air Transat

Air Transat is a Montreal-based airline. It was established in December 1986 with hubs in Montreal and four other Canadian cities. Winter services to the Caribbean, the USA, South and Central America, and – primarily in the summer months – to Europe are provided. The current airline fleet consists of Boeing 757s and Lockheed L1011s with additional airliners being leased during peak periods.

The Boeing 757 airliner appeared in the Air Transat fleet at the end of 1992 and the carrier now has five examples in the regular colours of the airline. Together with the L1011s, the Boeings are put into service on charter flights from Canada to the United Kingdom. In this photograph of C-GTSJ taken at Manchester in July 1996, the Boeing product is seen during the push-back operation prior to returning to Canada.

ABOVE:
During the winter peak period it is necessary for the airline to lease aircraft from other companies in order to meet additional schedules. Air Transat regularly provides flights from Canada to warmer climes during the winter months and European aircraft are often seen operating flights from the carrier's Canadian hubs. Boeing 737 series 400 C-GBIW was photographed in December 1997 at Fort Lauderdale about to return to Canada. This aircraft is one of two of the type leased to Air Transat from the United Kingdom airline Virgin Express, remaining in the colours of its owner during the leasing period, although with added Air Transat titles and tail logo.

LEFT:
During the previous winter, the airline leased a Boeing 757 to provide for the extra capacity the airline expected over the period. From December 1996 until the spring of 1997, the company put into service an aircraft leased from the Greek airline Venus. During this period the aircraft received the Canadian registration C-GTSU, and it was photographed in January 1997 proceeding for take-off from Fort Lauderdale.

The company introduced their updated colour scheme at the end of 1998 and the first airliner to receive the colours was Lockheed L1011 C-FTNC. The newly acquired livery reflects the company's involvement with other airlines, in particular Star Airlines of France. As other aircraft become due for repainting, this livery will be applied and it will also appear on newly delivered Airbus A330s. The TriStar was showing its new colours at Fort Lauderdale in January 1999.

Canada 3000

Owned by a team of Canadian investors, the airline began operations as Air 2000 Airlines in 1988. With its main base in Toronto, the carrier operates from a total of six Canadian cities flying to the US, the Caribbean Islands and the United Kingdom with a fleet of Boeing and Airbus Industrie airliners, all configured full economy class.

The first type of aircraft to join the Canada 3000 fleet was the Boeing 757, of which there are currently nine in service, including four extended range models. C-FOON is a regular model, photographed after arrival at London Gatwick in July 1997. The motif on the tail represents the airline's own tour operator, called C3 Leisure.

ABOVE:
The Airbus Industrie A320 was the second type of airliner to join the fleet of which six now carry the colours of the airline. The usual tail markings show the full name of the company as illustrated in the photograph of C-GVXB, shot whilst taxying to the Fort Lauderdale runway in December 1993.

RIGHT:
The latest type of airliner to enter service with Canada 3000 is the Airbus Industrie A330 twin-jet, two examples currently flying in the company colours. C-GGWA was the first to appear, joining the carrier in May 1998 and being put into service on the Canada to Europe flights soon afterwards. The airliner provides seating for 340 passengers, more than double that of the A320s. The recently built airliner was photographed about to land at Manchester in September 1998.

Royal

Royal Aviation, another of Canada's charter airlines, commenced operations from a Montreal base in April 1992, originally with Boeing 727s which were joined soon afterwards by Lockheed L1011s. The fleet has increased considerably over the years and now includes Boeing 737s and Airbus Industrie A310s. Services operate to several US destinations and the Caribbean, as well as northern summer services to the major Canadian cities.

Florida is one of Royal's winter destinations; regular flights are made to Fort Lauderdale, from where passengers transit to Port Everglades to join cruise liners, or simply spend a few days on the beach. Boeing 727 C-GRYP joined the Royal fleet in 1994 after flying in the colours of the Danish airline Sterling. It was photographed in December 1997 about to depart Fort Lauderdale.

Also departing Fort Lauderdale, in January 1998, is Airbus Industrie A310 C-GRYD, a recent addition to the fleet, having received the Royal colours in May 1997. The 265 seat airliner was operating a holiday charter service.

Kalitta

Kalitta American International Airways was formed in 1972 and received authority to operate international cargo charters in 1984. Its fleet consists of a large number of McDonnell Douglas DC-8s, Lockheed L1011s and Boeing 747s, the majority being configured to transport freight. However, the airline is also involved in the transportation of passengers and has four airliners in the fleet so configured; two 362 seat TriStars and two 476 seat Boeing 747s. These aircraft are regularly put into service on flights from North American cities to holiday destinations.

Lockheed TriStar N109CK is one of the L1011s configured for passenger use and was photographed whilst on finals for Las Vegas Airport in October 1997. No doubt the 'heavy' will be much lighter upon departure after its passengers have been relieved of their dollar bills!

American Trans Air

American Trans Air was formed in 1973 to manage the Ambassadair Travel Club. Today, this Indianapolis-based airline provides charter services to destinations throughout the US and points in Europe with a fleet of more than forty Boeing and Lockheed airliners.

ABOVE:
Lockheed L1011 N763BE photographed at New York JFK in October 1991 previously flew in the colours of Hawaiian Airlines and appeared in this temporary scheme upon being leased to 'Amtran' in June 1991. It was later purchased and repainted in the American Trans Air colours flying as N197AT.

RIGHT:
Seen again after repainting, N197AT was photographed whilst operating a charter flight to Greece in June 1998. The series 50 TriStar now carries the name 'Big Ed' and is about to land at Athens.

ABOVE:
A number of Boeing 757s fly in the airline's fleet, the majority of them being in the regular colours of the company. Photographed at Phoenix, Arizona, in October 1997 however, an example of the type is seen in the colours of the United Kingdom airline Monarch. N521AT was the latest 757 to be added to the 'Amtran' fleet and joined following a period of lease to the British airline.

LEFT:
The airline shortened its titles to ATA in January 1995. At that time it introduced a new corporate image promoting itself as America's true vacation airline, and adopted a new, leisure focused livery incorporating palm trees and sunshine. Illustrating this new colour scheme is Lockheed TriStar N196AT photographed in January 1998 about to depart Fort Lauderdale.

Apple Vacations

Apple Vacations is one of North America's largest tour operators with services originating in Chicago as Apple East and similar operations out of San Francisco as Apple West. The majority of flights operate during the northern hemisphere's winter period using aircraft supplied under contract by other airlines.

RIGHT:
During the winter period of 1994/1995, Apple Vacations put a Boeing 737 series 200 into service to operate charter flights in the Eastern United States. The aircraft was supplied by the Florida-based airline Carnival Airlines, and N73FS was photographed arriving at Miami in January 1995.

BELOW:
In the winter of 1997/1998, the company received aircraft from the Wichita, Kansas-based airline Ryan International, who had in turn leased four Airbus Industrie A320s from the United Kingdom charter airline Airworld Aviation. The four Airbuses were brand new at the time, two flying from Toulouse via Manchester to the States and two flying direct from the manufacturer. First to be delivered was G-BXKA which, like the others, was put into service in Airworld colours with the added Apple Vacations titles. Prior to flying over the Atlantic the aircraft put down in Manchester for a few hours to collect spares and equipment, and was photographed on a cold and damp November morning shortly before departure.

Express One

Express One International is a Dallas, Texas-based charter passenger airline, formed in 1980 to operate non-scheduled services under contract to companies in the USA, South and Central America and Europe. The present fleet consists of more than thirty airliners, the majority being Boeing 727s, including a number converted for cargo use, and three McDonnell Douglas DC-9s. All passenger carrying aircraft are configured full economy class with 113 seats in the DC-9s and 170 in the Boeings.

McDonnell Douglas DC-9 series 32 N945ML came to the airline on lease in January 1992 and continued in service for a further three years, during which time it was purchased by the carrier. Whilst operating a charter flight to Miami, the aircraft was photographed in June 1992 approaching one of the terminal's gates.

McDonnell Douglas DC-10 OH-LHA was originally delivered when new in 1975 to Finnair and since 1987 has been involved in several periods of leasing to other carriers. Commencing June 1993 it was leased to, and flew for 15 months for Express One to operate charter flights on long-haul routes. One of these services included flights from the US to Europe including Frankfurt/Main, and it is at this German city that the airliner was photographed in August 1993 about to return to the States.

Miami Air

Miami Air International is based in the Florida city of the same name, and commenced operations in October 1991. It was formed as a privately owned charter airline, and with a staff of 270, now operates seven Boeing 727 series 200 aircraft to international and domestic destinations in the Caribbean, North, Central and South America.

ABOVE:
Boeing 727 N804MA photographed in December 1995 on finals to Miami Airport shows a plain tail devoid of any markings other than the customary brown and green stripes. It does now however carry the name 'Lois'.

LEFT:
Photographed in December 1997 at the airline's Miami base making an approach from the east, Boeing 727 N806MA carries the name 'Ely' together with tail markings of the Florida Panthers team. Other aircraft in the Miami Air fleet also carry team markings.

Nomads

Nomads Inc. is a Michigan-based non-profit travel club and owns the aircraft it operates on behalf of its 6,000 members. The company was founded in 1965 when charter memberships were sold and their first aircraft, a DC-7 previously flown by Eastern Airlines, purchased. Flights are arranged for members of the club only.

The present aircraft operated by Nomads is a 1967 built Boeing 727 which previously flew for Lufthansa and Transair of Sweden. The tri-jet came to the travel club in 1993, and N727M was photographed in July 1996 whilst visiting one of the Portuguese Islands. Parked and awaiting departure, the aircraft is seen on the Funchal Airport ramp.

North American Airlines

This New York-based global-charter operator began flying in January 1990, providing flights from US cities, both for regular passengers and the US military. Originally, Boeing 737s and McDonnell Douglas MD-83s made up the North American fleet and these two types have now been joined by additional and newer aircraft.

ABOVE:
Boeing 757 N757NA joined the fleet in March 1990 and is the only extended range model of the three examples flown by the airline. This aircraft can be regularly observed at New York's JFK Airport and makes frequent flights to Miami, where it was photographed in December 1996 about to return north.

LEFT:
This aircraft was delivered new to North American in the summer of 1998 and was the airline's first Boeing 737 series 800. Photographed at Miami, N800NA is about to put down on runway 9L in December 1998.

Panagra

Panagra Airways is a Fort Lauderdale-based airline which started passenger charter operations in the summer of 1997 with a leased 200 series Boeing 727. The airline initially planned to operate to destinations within the USA, and between US airports, Mexico and the Caribbean.

ABOVE:
Boeing 727 N1969 was the first aircraft to be delivered to the airline, arriving at the company base in March 1997. In December 1998 it was photographed whilst at Opa Locka Airport.

RIGHT:
The whole of Panagra's fleet is illustrated in this spread, and the second 727 to be delivered was C-GKKF, joining the airline at the end of 1997. The colours carried by this Canadian-registered aircraft are those of the airline Greyhound Lines of Canada Ltd, with the addition of Panagra billboard style titles applied to the fuselage. The shot was taken in January 1999 at the company's Fort Lauderdale base.

Sun Country

Sun Country Airlines, the Minnesota-based regional and domestic charter carrier, started operations in 1983 following its formation by former Braniff employees in 1982. Services are currently provided within the US and to the Caribbean, Mexico and Europe. Seventeen airliners make up the Sun Country fleet, a mix of Boeing 727s and McDonnell Douglas DC-10s all operating in economy class configuration.

Boeing 727 N288SC is a 1973 built aircraft and joined Sun Country in 1994 after serving the previous 20 years with various other owners. The carrier's bright colours were photographed in June 1995 at Cancun as the airliner prepared to return to the United States with holidaymakers.

RIGHT:
Four of the carrier's DC-10 airliners are series '15' models, whilst another two of the type are '10' series. The latter have been in service with Sun Country since 1991 and were joined by the '15's in 1994. N573SC is a '10' model and was photographed in September 1995 about to depart Palma, Majorca. This particular aircraft no longer flies for Sun Country.

BELOW:
The airline's new colours appeared in the mid '90s and are seen here applied to series '15' N152SY photographed in October 1997 arriving at Las Vegas.

Sun Pacific

Sun Pacific International was established in 1995, its intention being to offer domestic and international charter services with a fleet of Boeing 727s. The airline is based in Tucson, Arizona, and now counts six 727s in the fleet, five being totally economy class configured, whilst the sixth is laid out for 53 passengers only and flown on behalf of a tour company.

Boeing 727 N79771 was the first aircraft to carry the Sun Pacific colours, entering service in January 1996. It was photographed between heavy showers on the Fort Lauderdale ramp in January 1997.

Tradewinds Airlines

Tradewinds International Airlines of Greensboro, North Carolina, was set up in 1969 and became an all-cargo airline in 1981 operating a Canadair CL-44 aircraft under the Wrangler Aviation name. The present title appeared in 1991 and the company now operates an international and domestic charter service. Its current fleet is totally made up of Lockheed TriStar L1011s. Passenger charter operations commenced in February 1998.

L1011 N75AA, originally a Gulf Air airplane was photographed in September 1998 whilst in push-back mode at Palma Airport, Majorca. *Allison Ann* was on lease to a European operator during the summer months of 1998 to provide flights to this Spanish island.

Allegro

Allegro Air is a Mexican passenger airline that has operated charter services since its formation in 1992. Flights are made mainly to destinations within Mexico, although the airline's small fleet of McDonnell Douglas DC-9/MD-83 and Boeing 727s also fly to North American points from the carrier's main base at Cancun.

Passengers from North America on inclusive tours to Mexican resorts often find themselves being transported on aircraft in the Allegro fleet. A returning flight to a North American airport in June 1995 was photographed about to depart Cancun. Boeing 727 XA-SXO is still under the control of the ground crew, who have just manoeuvred the airliner away from the terminal in readiness for take-off.

Air Atlanta

Air Atlanta Icelandic was formed in 1986 and entered the charter market in 1993, carrying passengers to most European holiday destinations. The airline is currently specialising in wet-leasing its fleet of Boeings and Lockheed TriStars to international airlines. Air Atlanta colours are to be seen at several European airports.

ABOVE:
All Air Atlanta aircraft are registered in Iceland and carry 'TF' prefix letters. Included in the current fleet are seven Lockheed L1011 airliners that have been re-configured to economy class since joining the airline. TF-ABE is a TriStar that came to the airline in 1995 following service with Cathay Pacific. When photographed in June 1996 it was transporting holidaymakers back to the UK and was about to come to a stand at Manchester.

RIGHT:
Air Atlanta also provides charter cargo services and two Boeing 737s in the fleet are equipped to provide for these services. Examples of the same type also fly in passenger configuration and during the summer of 1995 the airline leased TF-ABG and put it into service flying into and out of Frankfurt/Main. In August of that year, the twin-jet was photographed at that German city.

Air 2000

In July 1998, the First Choice Group, owners of Air 2000, acquired the travel company Unijet and became the owner of the United Kingdom's second largest charter airline. Operations started in April 1987 with a fleet of two Boeing 757s based at Manchester Airport, and this fleet has since expanded to exceed twenty Boeing and Airbus Industrie airliners. Services operate from fourteen United Kingdom and Eire airports to the traditional Spanish and Mediterranean destinations. Air 2000 operates over 100,000 hours of flying time each year, and their aircraft fly 2 million miles. In 1999, the airline received the award 'UK Best Charter Airline'.

Boeing 757 G-OOOA, the first aircraft to be delivered to Air 2000, was photographed in June 1995 about to depart Palma with returning holiday-makers to the UK. The aircraft is carrying the original colour scheme applied to the fleet; the 'First Choice' sticker positioned on the fuselage was added at a later date.

RIGHT:
Examples of Airbus Industrie A320s began to appear in Air 2000 colours in April 1992 and this type also operate flights to holiday destinations alongside the 757s. First to be delivered to the airline was G-OOAA, and this aircraft is illustrated in the photograph taken in September 1995 when landing at Palma.

BELOW:
To complete this trio of photographs taken at Palma Airport, Boeing 757 G-OOAD was shot in September 1998 upon arrival from London Gatwick with a full complement of holidaymakers. The Boeing is seen in the 'tapestry' livery introduced in October 1996 which is now to be seen on the majority of aircraft in the fleet, a colour scheme taking Air 2000 into the next millennium.

Airtours

Airtours International started operations from Manchester Airport in March 1991, at that time with a fleet of McDonnell Douglas MD-83 aircraft, operating inclusive tour and charter flights to major European holiday destinations. The airline is part of the Airtours Group, one of the United Kingdom's major tour operators, and its fleet of aircraft has increased dramatically, now including Airbus Industrie A320s, A321s, A330s, Boeing 757s and 767s. With the introduction of the larger airliners, the MD-83s were taken out of service. As well as providing flights within Europe, the company now flies to destinations in the US, the Caribbean and Australia. In 1996, its parent company acquired Premiair, the Danish charter airline, and aircraft of this company's fleet were repainted in Airtours colours.

Photographed in the year after it entered service with Airtours, McDonnell Douglas MD-83 G-GMJM is seen upon arrival at Manchester in April 1992.

Airtours' new colour scheme was introduced in January 1995, a Boeing 757 being the first aircraft to receive the new livery which incorporated the new red, green and yellow tail logo of Going Places, the travel agency owned by the airline. This logo is also applied to airliners in the Premiair fleet. Airbus Industrie A320 G-YJBM was photographed in this scheme in June 1995, seen taxying after arrival at Palma Airport.

The airline went 'BIG' during the summer of 1998 with the lease of a Boeing 747. A 200 model was leased from Air New Zealand from May until October to provide extra capacity on flights from the UK to Orlando, Florida and the Caribbean. Whilst in service with Airtours, the aircraft retained its New Zealand registration ZK-NZZ, its fuselage stripes and colours, but received the Airtours titles and Going Places tail logo. Photographed in May 1998 at Manchester, the Jumbo had just arrived from Orlando and after a 1½ hour turn-round, departed for the Caribbean.

Airworld/Flying Colours

Airworld Aviation commenced services in 1994 providing aircraft seats for Sunworld's inclusive tours to Mediterranean resorts from points in the UK. The airline later became part of the Thomas Cook Group and continued to provide similar services with its fleet of Airbus Industrie A320s and newly delivered A321s.

Flying Colours Airlines, a similar organisation to Airworld, was established in 1996 and commenced flying in March 1997 with a fleet of Boeing 757s which operated flights from the company's Manchester base to principle destinations in Europe. In June 1998, Sunworld, the owners of Airworld Aviation, acquired the

Flying Colours Group and the two airlines were merged under the ownership of the Thomas Cook Group, all aircraft later adopting the Flying Colours titles and flight numbers.

Until the delivery of their first A321 in April 1997, all flights operated by Airworld were made by their A320s. Manchester was one of the airports where aircraft were based, and flights also operated from Bristol, Cardiff and London Gatwick on a seasonal basis from May through October each year. During the winter months airliners were leased to Canadian and North American airlines. In the last month of operations in the 1996 season, Airbus A320 G-BVJV was photographed whilst parked at Manchester Airport.

ABOVE:
Photographed at Manchester in June 1997 shortly after the start-up of the airline, Flying Colours Boeing 757 G-FCLB was making an early morning arrival at the airport's Terminal 2 following a charter flight from Spain.

RIGHT:
Airbus Industrie A320 G-BXAT was added to the Flying Colours fleet on lease in May 1997 and was put into service bearing the full colours of the airline. There is one very small difference however, when compared with the photograph of the 757. The A320 was flying holidaymakers from Glasgow Airport and to denote its Scottish base, the dark blue flag of the airline's logo has been modified with a white cross of St Andrew. The Airbus was photographed at the gate at Palma Airport in September 1997 whilst being prepared for a return flight to Glasgow.

Air Scandic

Air Scandic was formed in May 1998 flying throughout the summer season to nine European destinations from Manchester Airport, principally for tour operators. Its main destinations are Spain, the Canary Islands and Greece, but when not operating on behalf of tour companies the airline offers its aircraft on lease to other carriers, being in a position to supply an airliner at short notice. Two Airbus A300s were acquired and put into service, each configured to carry 317 economy class passengers. At the start of the 1999 summer season, a third aircraft was obtained to provide extra capacity. An L1011 Tristar belonging to Aer Turas of Ireland was leased to Air Scandic for a period of six months carrying the Air Scandic colours.

Airbus A300 G-SWJW was photographed in May 1998 at Manchester in the original airline colours. A new livery appeared at the end of the 1998 charter season.

The new Air Scandic livery is totally different to the previous scheme. The designers have produced a livery with a holiday theme in mind. Airbus A300 G-SWJW is illustrated in the company's new colours and was photographed in May 1999 whilst parked at Manchester Airport.

Britannia

Britannia Airways is the largest passenger charter airline in the world and carries over 10 million passengers annually. Services commenced in May 1962 under the 'Euravia' name and 'Britannia' was adopted in 1964. The company is owned by the Thompson Travel Group and currently employs in excess of 3,000 staff, and has a fleet of over 30 airliners. The group established a German subsidiary in 1997 known as Britannia GmbH, and in 1998 acquired a Scandinavian holiday group which included the airline Blue Scandinavia. These two European subsidiaries are now operating in direct competition with existing German and Scandinavian charter airlines.

Britannia's services during the early 1980s were flown exclusively by Boeing 737s and as demand grew for more flights carrying ever-increasing numbers of passengers, the airline realised that larger aircraft were needed. The airline decided upon a programme of disposal of the 737s and replaced them with Boeing's larger models – the 757s and 767s. The latter was the first of the replacement types to be put into service and first flew in Britannia colours in February 1984. G-BKVZ was one of the first and was photographed in August 1984 about to depart Ibiza.

The 757s began to arrive towards the end of 1990 and provided services alongside the 767s and the remaining 737s. Whilst the latter type only provided seating for 130 passengers, the 757s and 767s gave the airline much more capacity with 235 seats and 328 seats respectively. This Boeing 757 was photographed in September 1994 whilst on approach to Ibiza.

BELOW:

The airline leased three Airbus Industrie A320s from May until October 1998 and these were used to carry holidaymakers on short-haul flights from the UK to Mediterranean destinations. A basic Britannia livery was applied, as shown in the photograph of EI-TLH taken in September that year when it was about to touch down at Palma Airport following a flight from the north of England's Leeds/Bradford Airport.

Although Britannia's fleet exceeds thirty aircraft, the carrier finds it necessary at times to lease aircraft from other companies in order to provide a complete summer programme. During the summer of 1997, a Boeing 767 was leased from Air New Zealand and operated flights into and out of Manchester. The aircraft carried the New Zealand registration during the period, and ZK-NBG was photographed in June 1997 departing Manchester.

Caledonian

Caledonian Airways is now part of the Thomas Cook Group following previous ownership by the Carlson Leisure Group, formally British Airtours Ltd. The airline operates in the charter market providing flights to the Mediterranean, Spain and Greece, together with long-haul flights to the US and Goa. The twelve-strong fleet is currently made up of Airbus Industrie, Lockheed and McDonnell Douglas types and these can be seen regularly at United Kingdom airports.

Whilst being a part of the British Airtours organisation, the airline included Boeing 757s in the fleet and G-BPEA was one example. However, this aircraft and others in Caledonian colours were later returned to British Airways and now fly for BA. When in Caledonian colours, the 757 was photographed in July 1990 being pushed back from its Manchester gate.

Airbus Industrie A320 G-BVYB is one of five of the type in use by Caledonian, and has been a member of the fleet since 1995. Photographed in October of that year, the European built airliner is under the control of the ground crew prior to its departure from Manchester.

Services to popular and long-haul destinations are performed by the carrier's Lockheed L1011s, its fleet of five being configured to carry 393 passengers. TriStar G-BBAI joined the Caledonian fleet in 1988, having previously served with British Airways and British Airtours and was photographed in August 1998 upon arrival at Rhodes.

European

European Aviation Ltd. started aircraft operations in 1994 when it obtained an Air Operator's Certificate with its subsidiary European Aviation Air Charter Ltd, an ad hoc charter airline. Commencing with two BAC 1-11 aircraft in 1998, the carrier had increased the fleet of 1-11s to 16 and operated them on a mix of ad hoc and wet leased charter flights. In addition, European Air Charter (EAL) purchased a fleet of Boeing 737s and immediately placed them on lease to the Belgian airline Sabena. The company's base is in Bournemouth.

BAe One-Eleven G-AVML was photographed in September 1995 about to depart Palma with a returning holiday charter flight to the United Kingdom. As an independent airline, EAAC operates no scheduled service of its own, is not affiliated to an inclusive tour operation and can therefore respond immediately to carriers' requests.

The 1-11 will continue as the core equipment for EAAC for at least two years. However, European Airlines are awaiting results of tests performed on one of its BAC 1-11 aircraft to establish a Stage III hush kit for the type. Should these tests prove satisfactory the airline will introduce Stage III compliant aircraft in service by year 2000 and the 1-11 will be assured for many more years beyond that date. G-AVML is again photographed in January 1999, this time at Opa Locka Airport, Florida, whilst visiting the USA for the tests.

Leisure International Airways

Leisure International Airways was a sister airline of Air UK (Leisure) set up to serve the holiday/leisure market. Operations started in April 1993 with a fleet of two Boeing 767 extended range models. The airline was wholly owned by the tour company Unijet and discontinued business in July 1998 following its acquisition by the First Choice Group, owners of Air 2000. The two aircraft now fly in Air 2000 colours. Air UK however continues to be operational and is now a subsidiary of the Dutch airline KLM, having been renamed KLM uk.

Boeing 737 series 400 G-UKLA was photographed in April 1995 about to depart Manchester. The livery is a modified version of that once carried on Air UK aircraft.

Boeing 767 G-UKLH was present at Manchester on the same April 1995 morning as the 737 and carries a similar livery, although the Air UK titles seen on the latter are replaced by Leisure International Airways on the wide-body. This 767 was the first to enter service with the airline and was used on flights to the Caribbean which would account for the name 'Caribbean Star'. Sister ship UKLI was given the name 'Atlantic Star'.

Monarch

Monarch Airlines was formed in 1967 and began operating flights in April 1968 with a fleet of Bristol Britannias. Thirty years later, the company now carries almost 5 million passengers annually to destinations in Europe, the US, the Caribbean and Far East. With a fleet in excess of 20 airliners, its aircraft are used to provide transportation for charter and inclusive tour packages for most of the UK's leading tour operators. The company base is at Luton but the Monarch colours are to be seen at most British airports.

Although Boeing 737s no longer feature in the Monarch fleet, when G-DHSW was photographed at Ibiza in August 1987, this series 300 airliner was one of six of the type in service with the airline.

The Airbus Industrie A320 was introduced into the Monarch fleet in 1993 and still provides sterling service on flights from United Kingdom airports to holiday destinations within Europe. G-MPCD is one of the type to carry Monarch colours and was photographed in June 1995 about to be pushed back from its gate at Palma Airport.

Charter flights are also performed by Monarch's small fleet of Airbus Industrie A300 airliners configured to carry 361 passengers. Four of the type are in use by the airline having been delivered new from the manufacturer. One example, G-MONS was photographed in July 1995 whilst proceeding for departure from Manchester.

With Monarch's introduction of charter flights to Florida and the Caribbean, a McDonnell Douglas DC-10 was added to the fleet to provide those services. G-DMCA arrived at Monarch in the spring of 1996 and is still in service providing flights to long-haul destinations from the UK. The series '30' machine was photographed proceeding along one of Manchester Airport's taxiways ready for take-off.

Peach Air

Peach Air started operations in the summer of 1997 providing charter flights from the United Kingdom airports Manchester and London Gatwick. The airline was part of the Caledonian Airways Group and leased airliners from the Icelandic airline Air Atlanta mainly to operate services to Mediterranean destinations. In November 1998, Peach Air discontinued operations.

Lockheed TriStar TF-ABM is one of four 1011s leased to Peach Air and was photographed in June 1998 during push-back operations at Manchester Airport

To provide extra capacity in the summer of 1997, the airline leased Boeing 737 series 200 G-SBEA from the London Gatwick-based charter airline Sabre Airways. The airliner was still flying for Peach Air when photographed in September 1998 on approach to Palma Airport.

Sabre

Sabre Airways started operations at the end of 1994 with two Boeing 737/200s taking over the services of the defunct airline Ambassador. The airline provides holiday charter flights from several United Kingdom airports to destinations mainly in Spain and the Mediterranean. The original 737s with which services were started have since been taken out of the fleet and replaced by Boeing 727s and a new series 800 Boeing 737.

Boeing 727 G-BNNI is a 1974 vintage airliner and previously carried the colours of the long departed Dan Air. When photographed in May 1995, the tri-jet was still in regular service transporting holidaymakers from Manchester and was about to depart to a Spanish destination.

53

Boeing 737 G-SBEB has at one time been leased to the charter airline Peach Air, but when photographed in June 1995 was operating a flight for Sabre in the regular colours of the airline. The twin-jet had just completed a flight from London Gatwick and is seen slowly taxying to a stand at Palma Airport.

Translift/
TransAer

Formerly known as Translift, this Dublin based airline has now changed its name to TransAer. The carrier commenced operations in 1992, flying on behalf of tour operators throughout Europe and the US, originally with a fleet of McDonnell Douglas DC-8s. These airliners have since been replaced and the carrier's fleet is completely Airbus aircraft of types A300 and A320. The change of name occurred in May 1997.

Airbus Industrie A320 EI-TLI photographed departing Manchester in August 1995 bears the logo and colours of All Leisure, an airline that operated during 1994, owned by a company which held a 49% stake in Translift at that time.

RIGHT:
Another Irish registered A320 to carry the Translift colours was EI-TLE, photographed in September 1995 when taking holidaymakers to Palma for a late summer vacation. The Airbus carries the regular Translift logo on its tail.

BELOW:
Following the name change in May 1997, aeroplanes began to appear with TransAer titles. The airline required additional aircraft to provide for the extra flights planned for the summer months, and leased an Airbus A300 from the North American carrier Carnival Airlines. The airliner was N228KW which retained the basic Carnival colours with the added tail logo and TransAer titles. When photographed in July 1997, the aircraft was about to depart Manchester.

Air Holland

Air Holland Charter BV was established in 1991 as an international charter passenger airline and operates from its base at Amsterdam's Schiphol Airport, with a fleet of Boeing 737s and 757s. The carrier's various destinations include most of the European holiday airports in Greece, Spain and the Canary Islands.

Boeing 757 PH-AHI was delivered new to the airline and has remained in the fleet except for short periods of lease to other carriers. Photographed in August 1994, the 219 seat airliner was making an early morning departure from Ibiza and was about to straighten up for immediate take-off.

Boeing 757 PH-AHK is also a member of the Air Holland fleet and was photographed at Manchester Airport's Terminal 2 in May 1998 upon push-back. The company colours have still to be applied to the aircraft following its addition to the fleet after transfer from the US airline, America West during the preceding month. Prior to flying in service with Air Holland, the aircraft was leased to the United Kingdom airline Britannia and operated services on its routes.

Air Belgium

Air Belgium was formed in 1979 as Abelag Airways and became Air Belgium in 1980. As an international charter airline it operates inclusive tour passenger charters to the Mediterranean and the Canary Islands with a fleet of Boeing 737s and Airbus A320s.

One of two of Air Belgium's Boeings is a series 400 model which was photographed in September 1995 when making an approach to Palma Airport. OO-ILJ is the largest of the airline's 737s, the second aircraft being a 300 series model.

Air Belgium introduced a new colour
scheme in the spring of 1997 which has
now been applied to both Boeing aircraft.
The series 300 model OO-ILK shows off
the new design in this photograph taken
at Rhodes in August 1998.

ChallengAir

ChallengAir is a Belgian international charter passenger airline and provides services with a small fleet of airliners, currently one Boeing 767 and one McDonnell Douglas DC-10. The company's aircraft are often leased out to other carriers during the peak summer months and can be observed carrying the titles of another airline.

ChallengAir's DC-10 OO-JOT entered the fleet in 1994 soon after the formation of the airline. It was photographed in August of that year making its way to a gate at Manchester's Terminal 2 whilst on lease to and operating flights on behalf of the United Kingdom airline Britannia.

Constellation

Constellation operated its first revenue earning flight on 1 July 1995 using the first of two Boeing 727s obtained from the French airline Air Charter. The two aircraft were based at Brussels and Palma, Majorca, with flights operating between those two points. These services continued in operation until the services were taken over by newly delivered Airbus A320s.

ABOVE:
Boeing 727 F-GCMV was photographed in September 1995 only a few weeks after the commencement of services. It is seen on approach to Palma Airport and will be recognised as a former Air Charter airplane, as part of their scheme still remains on the tail.

RIGHT:
With the introduction of the Airbus A320 to the fleet in May 1997, the airline presented its colours. OO-COF began operating flights from Brussels to various European destinations and it is at Athens that the newly delivered airliner was photographed in June 1998.

Sobelair

Sobelair is a charter subsidiary airline of the Belgian carrier Sabena. Established in 1946, the carrier has a dedicated fleet of aircraft and adds extra ones from the parent company in high season when circumstances dictate.

Boeing 737 OO-SDA was photographed in August 1994 at Ibiza Airport, lined up on the runway and ready to go. At that time the airplane was part of the Sobelair fleet but at the time of writing the Boeing was operating flights on behalf of Sabena.

Air Charter

Air Charter is a Paris-based airline providing passenger charter flights to world-wide destinations from over thirty French provincial cities. Formed in 1966 as a wholly owned subsidiary of the French national airline Air France, the carrier's small fleet of Boeing 737s and Airbus Industrie A310s and A320s is often expanded when aircraft in Air France colours are put into service to provide for additional capacity.

ABOVE:
Airbus Industrie A320 F-GLGE was photographed in September 1995 whilst operating a return flight to France. The Airbus had arrived at Palma earlier that morning and after a one hour turn-round collected its passengers and departed.

RIGHT:
One of Air Charter's earlier aircraft was a Boeing 737, F-GCLL, a series 200 model in the fleet of the French airline Euralair. The aircraft was being operated by Euralair on behalf of Air Charter when photographed at Frankfurt/Main in October 1989.

AOM

AOM French Airlines is an international and domestic charter passenger airline created by the merger of Air Outre Mer and Minerve at the beginning of 1992. Domestic services operate within France whilst international flights are made to French Polynesia, the West Indies and North America together with a variety of other charter destinations. The present fleet consists of Boeing 737s, and McDonnell Douglas MD-83s which serve the carrier's short-haul routes, along with McDonnell Douglas DC-10s which fly the long-haul routes.

ABOVE:
Photographed in January 1992 whilst still carrying the Air Outre Mer titles, McDonnell Douglas DC-10 F-ODLZ had just reached Miami as the sun began to set.

LEFT:
DC-10 F-GTDF shows the new regular colours of AOM but with the additional Cubana stickers which appear only on the port side. The airliner was operating flights on behalf of the Cuban airline and made regular flights from the United Kingdom to Cuba. Photographed in May 1997, the '10' is seen on the ramp at Varadero Airport following its non-stop flight from London Gatwick. After this brief stop the passengers bound for Havana re-joined the aircraft for the twenty minute hop to its final destination.

Air Toulouse

Air Toulouse International currently provides charter services with a fleet of Boeing 737s replacing a smaller fleet of aircraft including some Aerospatiale Caravelles which continued in service until 1997. The Boeings now provide transportation for the airline's passengers to destinations in France, the United Kingdom and the Mediterranean.

The Caravelles were put into service during the 1980s making regular appearances at many of the European airports when carrying holidaymakers from points in France. These services continued into the '90s and F-GHMU was photographed in August 1994 at Ibiza about to depart to France. At that time three of the type were flying in the company colours.

Belair

Belair Ile-de-France is a small French airline which commenced operations in September 1995 providing international and domestic charter flights. At the time of the launch only one aircraft, a Boeing 727, was in use, but the fleet gradually increased with the addition of a second Boeing 727 and a McDonnell Douglas MD-83.

Belair's first Boeing 727 to take to the sky was F-GGGR, seen in this photograph taken in August 1998 as it was about to land at Rhodes whilst operating a charter service from France.

Corsair

Corsair, formerly known as Corse-Air International, was established in 1981 and has its main base at the French capital city's Orly Airport. International and regional charter flights are operated to several world-wide cities, using a mix of short and long-haul Boeing airliners currently making up the Corsair fleet.

ABOVE:
Although carrying Corsair titles, Airbus Industrie A300 OY-CNK is in fact an airliner in the fleet of the Danish airline Premiair, and was being leased to the French carrier during the busy summer period. The airliner was photographed in September 1995 as it was preparing to line up for departure from Palma Airport.

RIGHT:
The current regular colours of Corsair are carried on Boeing 747 F-GLNA photographed in June 1998 about to land at Athens Airport. Six Jumbos make up the present Corsair fleet, all having previously served with other national airlines.

Star Airlines

Founded in 1995 as Star Europe, this airline was formed to provide transportation for a French travel company, and a Boeing 737 series 300 was put into service to operate those flights. The twin-jet was configured to carry 138 passengers. At the end of 1997 the airline was renamed as Star Airlines, and although a further two Boeings had been placed in service with the carrier, the type were later taken out of the fleet to be replaced by the larger Airbus A320, four examples of the type being put into service.

ABOVE:
The new batch of 737s put into the Star fleet were 400 models and they worked during the summer of 1997. Photographed in September of that year F-GRSB is seen taxying to the runway for departure from Palma.

LEFT:
The change of name has now taken place and the Boeings replaced by Airbus Industrie A320s. Majorca is still one of the destinations for the airline and in September 1998, F-GRSG was photographed whilst positioning for take-off from Palma.

Aero Lloyd

Aero Lloyd Flugreisen was established in 1980 and commenced international charter passenger services in March 1981, originally with a fleet of Caravelles, later to be joined by McDonnell Douglas series 32 DC-9s. From the carrier's bases in the German cities of Berlin, Frankfurt and Hamburg, flights are operated to most European sunspots. Over the following years newer aircraft have been added to the fleet, which has enabled the withdrawal of older planes, and Aero Lloyd now operates services with a modern fleet of almost thirty aircraft made up of McDonnell Douglas MD-83s, and Airbus Industrie A320 and A321 models.

McDonnell Douglas MD-83 D-ALLN was photographed in September 1995 whilst turning onto the runway at Palma Airport. 'Lima November' is in the colours introduced in 1986, replaced ten years later when new colours were introduced.

LEFT:
Upon the introduction of the Airbus A320 to the fleet, Aero Lloyd unveiled its new blue and red colour scheme and new tail logo. The first A320 was delivered in January 1996 closely followed by two more examples and a further three in 1997. When all A321 models on order are delivered to the airline, Aero Lloyd will have a total of seventeen Airbuses in service. D-ALAF is the sixth A320 to be delivered to the airline and was photographed in August 1998 about to depart Rhodes.

BELOW:
The newly introduced livery will also be applied to all McDonnell Douglas MD-83s as they become due for re-painting, and D-ALLV is one of the fleet to have been so treated. Photographed in August 1998, the 165 seat airliner is seen on the Rhodes Airport ramp.

Air Berlin

Air Berlin was formed in 1978 as an Oregon-based United States charter company, and was known at that time as Air Berlin USA. Whilst the head office of the company was located in Oregon, the airline operated out of Berlin's Tegal Airport on charter flights to the Canary Islands and Spain. In 1992, Air Berlin became a German company with headquarters in Berlin and at that time American aircraft identification markings were removed.

Whilst still under United States ownership, Boeing 737 series 300 N67AB was photographed about to depart Palma with a return charter flight to Germany. As well as carrying an American registration, the Boeing has the added inscription 'USA' after the titles on the fuselage and tail, along with a prominently placed American flag beside the main titles.

ABOVE:
Still with small 'AIR BERLIN' titling, Boeing 737 series 400 was photographed in September 1994 in a similar colour scheme to that in use earlier, but all American identification has now been removed, aircraft in the fleet now carrying German registrations. D-ABAF was photographed in September 1994 about to apply full power for take-off from Ibiza Airport.

LEFT:
When D-ABAE was photographed about to depart Rhodes in August 1998, the entire fleet of Air Berlin was made up of Boeing series 400 737s. The airliner shows the normal colours but titles have now been enlarged.

Condor

Condor Flugdienst is one of Germany's largest charter operators and is 100% owned by the country's national airline Lufthansa. Operations started in 1956 and the airline now provides charter passenger services to the Mediterranean and tourist resorts world-wide utilizing their extensive fleet of Boeing and McDonnell Douglas products. All aircraft with the exception of their nine Boeing 767 extended range models are configured for economy class travel.

McDonnell Douglas DC-10 D-ADLO was one of a fleet of five of the type in Condor's fleet when photographed in September 1995, and is seen about to touch down at Palma Airport bringing in a full load of German tourists. The DC-10s in service with Condor have now been reduced to three and the one illustrated has departed the fleet to find alternative service.

Photographed at Rhodes in August 1998 was Boeing 757 D-ABNF, one of eighteen series 200 models in Condor colours. 'November Foxtrot' is unique in that it carries the 'Rizzi Bird' markings applied to celebrate the company's 40th anniversary in 1996. It was expected that this livery would remain on this aircraft for four years.

Condor Flugdienst formed a low-cost subsidiary in the spring of 1998 and based the airline in Berlin. Airbus Industrie A320s already on order for delivery to the parent company were passed to the new airline and appeared in a revised colour scheme with the word 'Berlin' appearing beside the Condor titles. Six A320s fly in this scheme which is illustrated in the photograph of D-AICB taken upon arrival at Rhodes in August 1998.

Germania

Germania Fluggesellschaft is another of Germany's airlines providing international charter passenger services. Originally founded in 1978 and known as SAT with a base in Cologne, this carrier will be best remembered as the one with the green painted Caravelles which appeared at most of the European holiday destinations. In June 1986 the airline was renamed Germania and now has a base in Berlin from where its large fleet of Boeing 737s provides services to the Mediterranean, Spain and the Canaries.

ABOVE:
The Germania livery of the early '90s still uses green as a main colour, seen on Boeing 737 series 300 D-AGEI photographed in September 1995 when coming in to land at Palma.

RIGHT:
The carrier's first series 700 Boeing 737, of which it is expected to receive twelve in total, was delivered to the airline in March 1998. Three of the type will carry the colours of the German tour operator Touristik Union International and operate from Berlin and Stuttgart airports. D-AGEN was photographed in this colour scheme in August 1998 and had just arrived at Rhodes.

Hapag Lloyd

Hapag Lloyd Fluggesellschaft was established in 1972 and currently operates charter services to the Mediterranean, Eastern Europe and West Africa with a large and modern fleet of Boeing and Airbus Industrie airliners. The airline is a subsidiary of the large Hapag Lloyd shipping group.

ABOVE:
It is possible to observe the Hapag Lloyd colours at most of the European holiday destinations and Boeing 737 series 400 D-AHLR was photographed at Palma in September 1995 making one of its many visits to the island of Majorca.

LEFT:
Also photographed at Palma in September 1995, Airbus Industrie A310 D-AHLZ is seen arriving after completing a flight from Germany. The airliner is a 200 series model and one of four in the fleet to be fitted with winglets. The photographs in this spread illustrate the two types of aircraft currently flown by Hapag Lloyd.

LTU

LTU International Airways is without doubt the largest of Germany's charter airlines, operating from a base in Düsseldorf to more than seventy world-wide destinations. The current fleet list totals almost thirty airliners from the plants of McDonnell Douglas, Boeing and Airbus Industrie. At one time LTU provided services with a large fleet of Lockheed TriStar L1011s, but since the introduction of newer aircraft to the fleet this type has been taken out of service.

ABOVE:
When photographed at Miami in December 1987, L1011 D-AERT was one of nine TriStars in service with LTU and was the only type flown by the carrier. Miami is still one of the airline's long-haul destinations and services to this resort are now flown by MD-11s.

RIGHT:
The McDonnell Douglas MD-11s are also used to carry holidaymakers to the popular European sun-spots and the airline's four examples of the type are configured full economy with seating for 408 passengers. LTU make almost daily flights to the Balearic Islands from points in Germany during the summer season, and D-AERW was photographed in September 1995 about to depart Majorca's Palma Airport.

ABOVE:
The first of six Airbus Industrie A330s was delivered to LTU at the beginning of 1995 and these airliners too, are configured full economy with seating for 387 passengers, being used on various routes including the popular holiday destinations. D-AERF is the first A330 to receive LTU colours and was photographed in September 1998 about to depart Rhodes.

LEFT:
LTU Süd International Airways commenced operations in 1984 from a base in Munich and was a member of the LTU Group. Until its merger into LTU at the end of 1997 LTU Süd provided services to South America, the Far East and the US with a fleet of Boeing 757s and 767s which have since been integrated into the LTU fleet. Whilst still in LTU Süd colours, Boeing 767 D-AMUR was photographed in January 1995 arriving at Miami.

Falcon Air

Falcon Air is a Swedish airline and was formed in the 1960s as an air-taxi operator and now provides international, regional and domestic charter passenger and cargo services with a small fleet of Boeing 737 series 300 aircraft. Flights are operated to points within Sweden and to main holiday destinations from its main base in Malmö.

Boeing 737 SE-DPC can be configured to carry 142 economy class passengers or reconfigured as a pure freighter. When photographed in May 1998 on approach to Athens Airport, the twin-jet was carrying holidaymakers to Greek resorts.

Nordic East

Nordic East Airways flew charter passenger services to Europe, the Middle East and North Africa from its main base at Stockholm Arlanda Airport. Operations commenced in 1991 and services continued as Nordic East until July 1996 when the airline was renamed Nordic European Airlines. During the previous years and subsequently following the change of name of the airline, the carrier retained their fleet of two Boeing 737s and two Lockheed L1011s. Services continued for almost a further two years before the airline suspended operations in March 1998.

ABOVE:
Boeing 737 series 300 SE-DLO photographed in August 1995 at Frankfurt/Main had just left its gate at Terminal 2 and is seen proceeding for departure.

LEFT:
Although carrying the new Nordic European Airlines titles, Boeing 737 series 400 SE-DRR is seen with the tail colours of the Spanish airline Futura when photographed in September 1997 whilst flying for Nordic during the summer period. The airliner had discharged its passengers at Palma and was awaiting passengers for its return flight.

ABOVE:
Lockheed L1011 SE-DPX, also photographed at Palma in September 1997
had just arrived at the airport and was
following the instructions from the tower
to proceed to the gate to unload.

RIGHT:
Lockheed TriStar L1011 SE-DVM was
delivered to Nordic European in
November 1997 and was put into service
operating the carrier's long-haul routes, in
a temporary scheme without European
Airways titles. In January 1998, the
airliner was operating a North American
service from Stockholm and was
photographed about to depart Miami.

Novair

Novair was formed by a Swedish tour operator towards the end of 1997 and began operations providing flights between Sweden and the Canary Islands with two leased 300 seat TriStars which were joined later by an Airbus A320. A third Lockheed TriStar was added to the fleet during the first few months of 1998.

Two of Novair's Lockheed TriStars are 500 series models allowing the airline to provide flights to distant destinations without the necessity of stopping en route to re-fuel. SE-DVI is one of the long-range aircraft in the fleet and during the winter months 1998/1999 the carrier provided a weekly flight between Sweden and Florida. This photograph taken in January 1999 shows the aircraft about to depart Miami.

Premiair

Premiair A/S was established on 1 January 1994, created following the merger of two airlines – Conair of Denmark and Scanair of Sweden. The airline provides international and regional charter passenger services from its three main hubs located in Copenhagen, Oslo and Stockholm, transporting holiday-makers to the resorts in Greece, Spain and the Canaries. The airline's fleet currently comprises Airbus Industrie and McDonnell Douglas airliners, all configured economy class. In February 1996, the United Kingdom travel group Airtours acquired the airline and now has full control over Premiair.

ABOVE:
The majority of McDonnell Douglas DC-10s in the Premiair fleet are series '10' models, and only one of the type is a series '30'. OY-CNT is a '10' series and was photographed in June 1995 whilst operating a charter flight to Palma. The colours carried by the DC-10 were those in use by the airline prior to the acquisition by Airtours.

RIGHT:
One of the Airbus Industrie types flown by Premiair is the A300 model which are configured for almost 300 passengers. Three examples are currently in service and OY-CNL was photographed in September 1995 about to land at Palma.

LEFT:
Premiair aircraft began to receive new colours at the end of 1996 which are identical to those of the United Kingdom airline Airtours. Another DC-10, OY-CNU, photographed at Palma in September 1997 shows the new paint scheme applied to the Premiair fleet.

BELOW:
The latest type of aircraft to join the Premiair fleet is the Airbus A320 which began to appear in service towards the end of 1996. The airline has six examples which are leased to it from the United Kingdom carrier Airtours. Photographed in August 1998 whilst operating a summer charter service, OY-CNM is at Rhodes Airport.

Sterling

The original Sterling Airways went bankrupt in 1993 and a new Sterling European Airways was formed at the end of that year, starting operations in May 1994. This Danish company is based in Copenhagen and currently operates an all Boeing fleet of 727 and 737 airliners. A number of the 727s in service are operated as freighters on behalf of TNT. International charter flights are also made to the main European holiday destinations.

Boeing 727 OY-SBE was photographed in December 1990 in the original Sterling Airways colours. At that time the aircraft was on winter lease to the Central American airline Lacsa, and was operating out of Miami.

LEFT:
With the change of name following the re-launch of the airline came a new colour scheme. The new Sterling colours are to be seen at most of the major holiday destinations and Rhodes is one airport into which the airline regularly flies. Photographed at this Greek tourist spot in August 1998, Boeing 727 OY-SCC had just arrived from Denmark.

BELOW:
To commemorate the introduction of the series 300 Boeing 737 into the Sterling fleet in the summer of 1998, the airline adopted a new 'beach ball' colour scheme, and the new livery is illustrated in the photograph of Boeing 737 OY-SEB about to depart Palma in September 1998.

Transswede

Transswede Airways was a Swedish charter passenger airline and operated from a Stockholm base providing flights to Europe and the Mediterranean. Operations commenced in April 1985 and continued under this name until becoming known as Braathens Sverige in 1998, a subsidiary of the Norwegian airline Braathens SAFE. The current fleet of the re-named airline consists of Fokker 100s and one Boeing 737.

ABOVE:
Operating under the Transswede name in 1995, McDonnell Douglas MD-87 SE-DHI was photographed in June of that year upon arrival at Palma Airport. The flight is actually a Transswede Leisure service, a subsidiary of Transswede Airways formed to operate the parent's international charter services.

RIGHT:
Also photographed at Palma in September 1995 was McDonnell Douglas MD-83 SE-DHN, sitting on the ramp whilst the cleaners and maintenance crew perform their duties prior to the return journey to Scandinavia.

Balair CTA

Compagnie de Transport Aerien (CTA) was formed in September 1978 as a partly owned subsidiary of the airline Swissair, and provided charter and inclusive tour flights from its base in Geneva. The airline at one time had a fleet made up entirely of Caravelles which were used to transport passengers to the destinations in the Middle East and Europe. These airplanes were taken out of service towards the end of the 1980s and replaced by McDonnell Douglas MD-87s.

Balair was formed in 1953 and was also involved in passenger charter operations. The company was partially owned by Swissair and operated similar services to CTA. The two airlines were merged in 1993 to form Balair CTA and the airliners of each company received a common title and revised livery. As Balair CTA, the airline ceased operations in 1995, but restarted as Balair CTA Leisure in 1997 with a reduced fleet of Airbus Industrie airliners.

ABOVE:
McDonnell Douglas MD-87 HB-IUA was photographed in August 1992 with the CTA titles and livery which included the wording 'Membre du Groupe Swissair' following the main titles. The airliner is seen approaching its stand at Ibiza following a flight from Switzerland.

LEFT:
Included in the original Balair fleet was a McDonnell Douglas DC-10 which flew services on long-haul passenger charter flights. HB-IHK is a series 30 model providing fourteen years of service with Balair prior to the merger with CTA. It was the airline's only wide-body airliner and was photographed in May 1990 about to depart John F Kennedy Airport, New York.

A new livery was applied to Balair's airliners with a much bolder and more modern appearance. McDonnell Douglas MD-82s and '83's were part of the Balair fleet in the early 1990s and provided flights to European holiday destinations. HB-INB is an '82' model and was photographed at Ibiza in August 1992.

RIGHT:
Following the 1993 merger of the two airlines, the fleet list of the new carrier consisted of McDonnell Douglas MDs and Airbus Industrie A310s, although when services were discontinued in 1995, the MDs were not reintroduced. When the airline commenced flying again in the autumn of 1997, Airbus A310s did however, find their way into the fleet again, and HB-IPM, incorporating the new title of the airline Balair CTA was photographed in January 1998 whilst operating a charter flight to Miami.

Edelweiss

Edelweiss Air is a Swiss charter carrier formed to provide increased competition in that sector and two McDonnell Douglas MD-83s were delivered at the beginning of 1996 to provide services. These aircraft were later joined by a third of the type. Flights are made from Zurich to the majority of the popular European holiday destinations. The three MD-83s were replaced by three Airbus Industrie A320s during 1999.

The second MD-83 to enter service with the airline was HB-IKM which arrived at Zurich on delivery in March 1996. The twin-jet is illustrated in the photograph taken at Rhodes in August 1998.

TEA Switzerland

TEA Switzerland commenced international charter operations in March 1989 as part of the TEA Group of airlines flying to European destinations with a small fleet of Boeing 737s. In March 1998, the airline was taken over by the United Kingdom based airline easyJet and continued operating as TEA Switzerland until changing its name to easyJet Switzerland in November of that year.

Whilst operating a charter flight from Switzerland in September 1998, Boeing 737 series 300 HB-IIB was photographed about to take off from Palma. This Spanish island, together with the islands of Greece, were visited frequently by the Boeings in the company fleet during the summer months.

Air Europa

Air Europa (Air Espana) is the operating title of this Spanish-based charter airline, which commenced operations in November 1993. With a fleet of Boeing 737s flights are made to most European destinations, whilst the Boeing 757s and 767s in Air Europa colours provide transportation to more distant points including the Far East, the Dominican Republic and the Caribbean.

ABOVE:
A member of the Boeing 757 fleet is EC-FEF which was still in the original livery when photographed in September 1995. The airliner was making a late afternoon departure from Palma and is just about to enter the runway for take-off.

LEFT:
Another Boeing 757 in the Air Europa fleet is turned out in a modified livery shown in the picture of an unidentified airliner photographed at Palma in June 1995.

Air Plus

Air Plus Comet started operations in March 1997 with two Airbus A310s providing transportation for tour operators on routes between Spain, the Caribbean and the US. The airline is based in Madrid and has since increased its fleet of A310s to three. When the necessity arises, the airline leases its aircraft to other carriers.

Airbus Industrie A310 EC-GOT had been leased to a United Kingdom charter operator when photographed in July 1998 and was departing Manchester Airport's Terminal 2 bound for a Spanish destination.

BCM

This Spanish charter airline commenced operations in November 1996 with a service from Palma, Majorca to the north of England airport Teeside. The airline was owned by a person with the initials BCM. During 1997, the airline put three leased Airbus Industrie A320s into service providing charter flights from Spain to several European airports, which continued to operate throughout the holiday season until all flights were discontinued at the beginning of January 1998.

Airbus Industrie A320 EC-GNB shows the second livery to be applied to the company's fleet, photographed in September 1997 when about to land at Palma on completing a flight from Germany.

Iberworld

Following the demise of BCM Airlines, a new Spanish charter company was formed by Iberjet, and the new airline Iberworld commenced operations in the summer of 1998 providing similar services to those performed by BCM. Iberworld's aircraft are leased from the same source as those supplied to BCM.

As was the case with BCM Airlines, Iberworld's fleet is also totally comprised of A320s. The Spanish islands are the main destinations of the airline and one of the carrier's Airbuses, EC-GLT, was photographed in September 1998 as it slowly taxied to the runway for take-off from Palma. The airliner illustrated previously flew in the colours of BCM Airlines.

LTE

LTE International Airways is a subsidiary of the German organisation LTU and is based in Spain, from where its fleet of three Boeing 757s provides international charter passenger flights, mainly to European destinations. The airline has been operational since 1987.

Boeing 757 EC-ETZ was photographed in August 1992 about to depart Ibiza with returning tourists. The livery carried by LTE aircraft will easily be recognised as that of its parent LTU.

Spanair

Spanair is an international and domestic charter passenger airline with a main base and hub at Palma Airport on the island of Majorca. Operations commenced in March 1988 and from the carrier's other hubs at airports on the Spanish mainland and Canary Islands, a comprehensive list of destinations are served by a modern fleet of McDonnell Douglas and Boeing airliners. Flights are made to over 100 European cities together with international services to the US, Mexico and Central America.

ABOVE:
McDonnell Douglas MD series twin jets are put into service on the majority of Spanair's European routes and all those in service provide economy class seating only. Photographed in August 1992 upon arrival at Ibiza Airport, MD-83 EC-ESJ still flies for Spanair and now carries the registration EC-FZC.

RIGHT:
The international services operated by Spanair are flown by the two Boeing 767s currently in Spanair colours. Both aircraft joined the airline in 1991 and the series 300 extended range models enable the carrier to provide non-stop flights from the Spanish mainland and islands to destinations in the Americas. Services currently operate from Madrid to Washington DC, and Rio de Janerio. One of the airline's 767s, EC-FCU, was photographed in September 1995 on final approach to Palma.

Victoria

Victoria Airlines began charter services in August 1998 from its Verona base, offering flights from Italian cities to holiday destinations in Europe. Two Airbus Industrie A320s were leased and put into service, each with different appearances. Services operated for only a short time however, as the two aircraft returned to their respective owners in October 1998.

One of the aircraft operated by Victoria Airlines was leased to it by the Turkish airline Onur Air. The airliner retained its colours and registration TC-ONF during the leasing period and merely had the Victoria Airlines stickers applied to the fuselage. The airliner was photographed in that condition at Rhodes in August 1998.

Volare

Volare Airlines is a newly formed Italian charter airline established in 1997 and currently operates a fleet of three Airbus Industrie A320s from a Verona base to destinations in Russia, the Middle East and points in Europe. The aircraft are leased and carry French registrations.

One of Volare's A320s was visiting the Greek island of Rhodes when the picture of F-GJVX was taken in August 1998. This aircraft was the first to join the airline and flew regularly to Rhodes on a weekly charter. The returning passengers had already boarded when the photograph was taken and the airliner was about to taxi for take-off.

Egretta

Egretta Air Company was one of the Czech Republic's charter airlines and was formed in 1991. Its two largest airliners were Soviet built Il62s which provided charter flights from the company's base in Prague to various holiday destinations. The airline discontinued services at the end of 1997 and the two Il62s were sold.

Photographed whilst operating a charter flight in September 1997 only a few weeks before the company's demise, is Il62 OK-OBL, seen about to depart Palma on a returning holiday service.

Fischer

Fischer Air was established to operate exclusively for the tour operator Fischer, its first flight in April 1997 being a charter service from the carrier's Prague base to Palma, Majorca. Two Boeing 737 series 300 aircraft were delivered to the airline during the first month of operations, and both are still providing transportation for the tour company's clients.

Boeing 737 series 300 OK-FUN was the second of the two to be put into service with Fischer and was photographed in August 1998 at Rhodes.

VIA

VIA vita est commenced operations in the summer of 1990 transporting holidaymakers from European cities to the beaches and sunshine of Bulgaria. From its base in Varna, the carrier originated services with Tupolev 154s and the Soviet built airliners are still operating the flights, with six examples of the type currently in service.

Tupolev 154 LZ-MIG was the first aircraft to enter service with VIA and was delivered new to the airline in 1990. Bulgaria is a destination for many of the United Kingdom's holidaymakers and the airline makes frequent flights between the two countries during the summer months. It was photographed on one of those flights in the summer of 1997 and is seen arriving at Manchester Airport.

Pegasus

Pegasus Airlines is an Istanbul-based international charter passenger carrier and has been operating services since April 1990 when two Boeing 737/400 aircraft were obtained. The airline has increased its fleet over the years and has remained a Boeing operator, currently with eight examples in service. Flights originate from a number of Turkish airports, mainly to European destinations in Germany, Finland, Norway, France, Holland and the UK. The aircraft in the Pegasus fleet are also leased to other airlines as and when required.

Whilst operating a return charter flight to Turkey in May 1996, Boeing 737 series 400 TC-AFM was photographed negotiating the Manchester Airport taxiways. The aircraft had departed from the airport's Terminal 2 and congestion had made it necessary for the Boeing to pass through the Terminal 1 ramp area.

Sun Express

Sun Express Airlines is a Turkish international charter passenger airline operating a small fleet of Boeing and Airbus Industrie aircraft on routes from Turkey to most of the countries in Europe. Services commenced in April 1990 with one Boeing 737, two more of the type being added during the following year. Sun Express is jointly owned by Lufthansa and Turkish Airlines.

ABOVE:
Boeing 737 series 300 TC-SUR was photographed in October 1992 about to depart Frankfurt/Main. There are frequent flights between Turkey and Germany and it is possible to observe Sun Express aircraft at this airport regularly.

LEFT:
Airbus Industrie A320 EI-TLF is owned by an Irish aircraft leasing company and is put into service by a variety of airlines as and when required. Sun Express found the need to obtain additional aircraft during the 1995 summer peak and put the Airbus into service on its routes. During the four month lease to Sun Express the airliner received the carrier's logo and titles and was photographed in August 1995 at Frankfurt/Main.

Eurocypria

This Cyprian airline commenced operations in March 1992 from bases at Larnaca and Paphos Airports, providing international and regional passenger charter flights with two Airbus Industrie A320s, later joined by a third of the type. The three A320s are still in service with the airline, providing transportation for holidaymakers from Germany, Scandinavia and the United Kingdom travelling on inclusive tours to Cyprus.

Airbus A320 5B-DBB was one of the first two of the type to enter service with Eurocypria and was photographed in March 1997 on final approach to Manchester after completing a flight from Paphos.

Pharaoh Airlines

Pharaoh Airlines is a Cairo, Egypt-based charter airline and entered into the market in July 1998 with a Cairo to Istanbul flight. The carrier's initial plan is to operate a Boeing 737 series 200 on charter flights from Cairo to Greece and Turkey.

The Boeing 737 put into service by Pharaoh Airlines is one originally flown by the French airline Euralair, and was photographed in August 1998 after arrival at Rhodes Airport. The aircraft is now re-registered SU-PMA and was making one of its first appearances in Greece. It is expected that a second 737 may join the fleet, appearing in similar colours but with a different Pharaoh's head on the tail.

Alak

Alak-Air Leasing Company began operations in 1992, providing back-up aircraft for some of the main Russian carriers. It now operates world-wide charter flights from its Moscow base. The airline's entire fleet is Soviet built, comprising examples from the Tupolev and Ilyushin plants.

Tupolev 154 RA-85713 was photographed in September 1995 as it lifted off the runway at Palma Airport. For the past few years Majorca has been a popular spot for Soviet people and this aircraft, together with those in the fleet of the national airline Aeroflot, are frequent visitors during the summer months.

Ural Airlines

Ural Airlines is a Russian charter passenger and cargo airline based in the city of Ekaterinburg, situated in the Urals. The fleet of the airline is completely Soviet built and comprises three types – Antonov, Tupolev and Ilyushin, the latter two types being passenger carrying aircraft. Charter flights are made mainly to Europe, the Middle East and South East Asia.

A total of sixteen Tupolev 154 aircraft are included in the Ural Airlines fleet, all but two being configured full economy class. Flights from the CIS are often made to the Emirates and an example of the type was put into service during April 1998 when RA-85432 was photographed whilst parked on the ramp at Sharjah Airport.

ASA

African Safari Airways was created in 1967 to serve Kenya's tourist industry. It operates inclusive tour passenger charters to the game parks of East Africa. Flights are made from several European airports in Switzerland, Germany and the United Kingdom.

ABOVE:
The McDonnell Douglas DC-8s have been featured in the ASA fleet for some considerable time, and photographed in August 1992 at Frankfurt/Main, HB-IBF was being prepared to receive passengers for travel to Kenya. The airline's base is in Switzerland and included in the tail design of the DC-8 is the Swiss flag.

RIGHT:
The DC-8s are no longer to be seen in ASA colours and the airline put its first wide-body into service at the end of 1992. The carrier remained a customer of McDonnell Douglas and commenced operating its services with one of their DC-10s, and PH-DTL was photographed, again at Frankfurt/Main, as it arrived on an afternoon flight.

Daallo Airlines

Daallo Airlines was established in 1991, commencing operations with a Cessna Caravan in the sector between Djibouti and Hargeysa. It has now become the premier airline in Somalia and Djibouti, operating regular services to the United Arab Emirates, Jeddah and various destinations in Somalia. The company now has a fleet of six aircraft, which are in service on the carrier's new passenger and cargo charter flights within Africa.

With the UAE emerging as a top-notch tourist destination, Daallo Airlines sees the area as a tremendous business opportunity to provide charter flights, and a plan is underway to establish an air charter subsidiary company in Sharjah. Tupolev 154 EY-85691 was photographed in April 1998 at this United Arab Emirates airport.

Transmile Air

Transmile Air Services is a Malaysian charter passenger and cargo airline operating out of a Kuala Lumpur base. Operations started in November 1993 with services mainly centred around the Far East area. A Boeing 737 in the airline's fleet provides flights on behalf of a holiday company.

McDonnell Douglas DC-10 N833LA was leased to the airline from Laker Airways for a period of three months during 1998 to operate Hadj flights. Throughout the duration of the lease the airliner remained in the basic Laker colours with the addition of Transmile Air titles and tail logo. The series '30' model was photographed in April 1998 whilst visiting Sharjah.